IT'S AMAZING!
SUPERHEROES

Annabel Savery

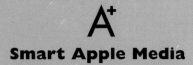

Smart Apple Media

Published by Smart Apple Media, an imprint of Black Rabbit Books
P.O. Box 3263, Mankato, Minnesota 56002
www.blackrabbitbooks.com

Printed in the United States of America at Corporate Graphics, North Mankato, Minnesota.

Published by arrangement with the Watts Publishing Group LTD, London.

Library of Congress Cataloging-in-Publication Data
Savery, Annabel.
Superheroes / Annabel Savery.
p. cm.—(It's amazing!)
Includes index.
ISBN 978-1-59920-692-9 (library binding)
1. Superheroes—Juvenile literature. 2. Comic strip characters—Juvenile literature. I. Title.
PN6725.S365 2012
741.5'0973--dc23
                    2011030545

Planning and production by Discovery Books Limited
Managing editor: Laura Durman
Editor: Annabel Savery
Designer: Ian Winton

Picture credits: Alamy: p. 4 (AF Archive), p. 7 bottom (Pictorial Press Ltd), p. 9 (AF Archive), p. 10 (AF Archive), p. 17 (AF Archive), p. 23 (Photos 12), p. 25 (Photos 12), p. 28 (Moviestore Collection Ltd); Getty Images: p. 6; Photoshot: p. 5 (Starstock), p. 8, p. 11 (Starstock), p. 13, p. 14, p. 16, p. 18 (Starstock), p. 19, p. 22, p. 24, p. 26, p. 29; Shutterstock Images: p. 7 top (all Carsten Reisinger), p. 27 top and p. 31 (Faiz Zaki), p. 27 bottom (DDCoral); Cartoon Network: Title, p. 20 left, p. 20 right, p. 21 (BEN 10 and all related elements are TM and © Cartoon Network. All rights reserved.)
Cover: IstockPhoto.com: serow.

PO1602 / 4-2013

9 8 7 6 5 4 3 2

CONTENTS

All words in **bold** appear in the glossary on page 30.

SUPERHEROES!

Superheroes are people from stories who have special powers. Some of these special powers include being able to fly, being incredibly strong, and being able to heal themselves.

Spider-Man

Superheroes use their powers for good. They help to protect people by solving crimes and catching criminals. Superheroes often rescue people, too (left).

Superheroes get their powers in different ways. They might be born with them or find they have them after an accident. Other superheroes use **gadgets** to protect themselves and help them to win fights.

Secret Identities

Most superheroes have **secret identities**. They hide their faces when they rescue people so that they cannot be recognized. Bruce Wayne (below) wears his Batman costume so that people do not know who Batman really is.

THE COMICS

Most superheroes were originally created for comics. There are two main superhero comic book makers: DC and Marvel.

DC and Marvel comic books tell all sorts of exciting adventures of different superheroes. They are written like a **storyboard**, so that you can read them like watching a movie.

A Marvel comic book

WHAM!!

KAPOW!!

BOOM!

ARRRRGH!

When the superheroes fight evil criminals, the comics use words like KAPOW, WHAM, and ZAP to represent the sounds.

BOOOOM!

So Many Superheroes

DC and Marvel have created hundreds of superheroes. As well as Superman (see pages 8–9) and Spider-Man (see pages 10–11), other great characters include The Flash, Aquaman, and Daredevil (left).

SUPERMAN

Superman's human name is Clark Kent. Although he looks human, he is actually an alien from the planet of Krypton. His alien name is Kal-El.

Superman (below) has many superpowers. He is fast, powerful, and can fly. He also has supervision which means he can see through things and see things that are a long way away.

Kryptonite

There is only one thing that can really hurt Superman—kryptonite. This is a radioactive mineral that was created when his home planet was destroyed. It takes away Superman's powers and can even kill him.

Kryptonite

Superman's **nemesis** is Lex Luthor (right). He is a rich scientist who has always hated Superman. He tries to destroy Superman using kryptonite.

SPIDER-MAN

Spider-Man's real identity is Peter Parker. He was an ordinary boy until he was bitten by a radioactive spider. The bite gave him spiderlike powers.

Spider-Man (above) can shoot webs from his wrists. He uses them to swing from tall buildings and to escape from danger. He can also cling to any surface and use his "spider senses" to react quickly to danger.

Spider-Man has many enemies, but the main one is the Green Goblin. He is very powerful, but is also **insane**. Other enemies are Dr. Octopus (above) and Venom.

Famous Words

Spider-Man's famous line is "With great power comes great responsibility." It appeared in the first Spider-Man comic.

WONDER WOMAN

Wonder Woman is the most famous female superhero. She is Princess of the Amazons and has many superpowers.

Wonder Woman is superstrong and superfast. She also has special powers, such as being able to talk to animals and even superquick typing!

Wonder Woman uses special equipment. She wears silver bracelets that **deflect** bullets. She has a tiara that can be thrown at enemies. She also carries a special rope called the "Lasso of Truth." Once inside it, a person cannot escape and can only tell the truth.

IT'S AMAZING!

As well as all her other equipment, Wonder Woman also has an invisible airplane!

Tiara

Silver
bracelet

Lasso
of Truth

BATMAN

Batman protects the people of Gotham City. His real name is Bruce Wayne. He is also known as "The Caped Crusader."

Bruce Wayne is a very rich man. His strength and power come through training rather than **supernatural** abilities.

Batman wears a special suit made of tough material. He speeds around in an **armored** car called the Batmobile. It has rocket boosters to make a quick getaway!

The Bat-Signal

When Batman is needed, the Gotham City police shine a searchlight with a bat symbol into the sky for Batman to see.

Batman's main enemy is the Joker. He is very clever and evil. The Joker tries to kill Batman and the people who are close to him. Batman has other enemies that are just as scary, such as Catwoman and the Riddler.

THE HULK

The Hulk was an ordinary scientist named Dr. Bruce Banner until he was accidentally hit by the gamma rays from a bomb.

The bomb turned Bruce Banner into a superhero. When Bruce is angry, he changes into the Hulk (below). The Hulk is enormous and incredibly strong. He is also bright green! The Hulk's strength increases with his temper, but even though he gets angry, he is still one of the good guys.

The Hulk's strength is not his only power. He can stand temperatures as hot as the sun and survive in space or underwater without any equipment. His body also heals itself after an injury.

A Nearby Nemesis

Bruce Banner has a girlfriend named Betty Ross (below, left). Unfortunately, her father is General Ross (below, right), the Hulk's archenemy.

IRON MAN

The man behind the Iron Man suit is Tony Stark. He is a genius and the owner of a company called Stark Enterprises.

Tony Stark was kidnapped by an enemy, and his captors tried to force him to make them a powerful weapon. Instead, he made the Iron Man suit (right) in secret, and used it to escape. Later, he uses the suit to protect the world from powerful criminals.

Heart-Stopping!

When he was kidnapped, Tony Stark was injured, and so he has to wear a chest plate to keep his heart working. The chest plate is also the battery for the suit.

Battery

The Iron Man suit gives Tony Stark all his power. It is made of very tough material to protect his body. The palms of his hands (above) can fire **repulsor rays** at enemies. The suit also has powerful rocket boosters in the feet so that Iron Man can fly!

BEN 10

Ben 10 is a favorite superhero with kids everywhere!

Ben 10 is actually a boy named Ben Tennyson (below). Ben uses a wristwatch called an Omnitrix to turn himself into different aliens with superpowers.

Omnitrix

Ben is helped by his Grandpa Max and his cousin Gwen. They go on adventures together. He uses his powers to fight criminals. He often gets into mischief on his adventures, too!

Ben 10 was created in 2005 by a group called "Man of Action." The character is so popular that there are now Ben 10 cartoons, movies, and video games.

Powerful Aliens

All of Ben's aliens have superpowers. For example, Nanomech (right) can shrink to a tiny size, fly, and shoot blasts of energy.

THE FANTASTIC FOUR

The Fantastic Four are a group of superheroes who work together. They have no secret identities, so everybody knows who they are.

Reed Richards – "Mr. Fantastic"

Cosmic Rays

Originally, the Fantastic Four were space shuttle pilots. They were hit by cosmic rays and their superpowers came from this accident.

Each of the Fantastic Four has a different superpower. Mr. Fantastic can bend himself into any shape. His wife, Susan Storm, is the Invisible Woman, and her brother, the Human Torch, can burst into flames and fly. Their friend, the Thing, has stone-like flesh which means he is very strong.

Susan Storm – "The Invisible Woman"

Johnny Storm – "The Human Torch"

Reed Richards – "Mr. Fantastic"

Ben Grim – "The Thing"

THE X-MEN

The X-Men are another group of superheroes who work together.

The X-Men's powers come from **genetic mutations.**
For example, Wolverine (above, center) was born
with animal senses, claws that spring out of his
hands, and the ability to heal from any injury.

One of the X-Men is Storm (below). She can control the weather and is a skilled fighter.

Professor Charles Xavier is the leader of the X-Men and the man who brought them together. He created a training center for them in his mansion so that they could learn to use their powers for good.

IT'S AMAZING!

To start with, there were only five X-Men. Now there are nearly 100!

TRANSFORMERS

The Transformers are a group of alien robots.

There are good Transformers and bad Transformers. The Autobots are the good robots and the Decepticons are their enemies.

The Autobots come from a planet called Cybertron. They are led by Optimus Prime. His team of Autobots on Earth are Bumblebee, Ratchett, Ironhide, and Jazz.

**Autobot
Optimus Prime**

Both the Autobots and the Decepticons are **humanoid** robots. However, they can transform into machines, such as vehicles or aircraft. Bumblebee (left) transforms into a yellow car (below).

Bumblebee

Toy Transformers

Transformers started as a line of toys made by a company called Hasbro. They were so popular that they were made into Marvel Comics series, cartoons, video games, and movies.

SUPERHERO MOVIES

Many movies have been made about superheroes. Here are some facts about them that you might not know.

The first blockbuster superhero movie was about Superman. It was made in 1978. A more modern movie was made in 2006 called *Superman Returns*, and a new movie will be coming out in 2013 called *Superman: Man of Steel*.

The 2008 Batman movie *The Dark Knight* made an incredible amount of money. It earned $158 million on its opening weekend in US theaters and $22 million in the UK.

Batman and the Joker in *The Dark Knight*.

IT'S AMAZING!

Between 2002 and 2007, three Spider-Man movies were made. The first cost $138 million to make. The next two movies were even more expensive, costing $200 million and $258 million!

GLOSSARY

Amazons a race of tall, strong, and fierce female warriors in Greek mythology

archenemy a main enemy

armored covered with or made of hard, protective metal

captor a person who takes someone else prisoner

cosmic rays waves from outer space

deflect to cause something to change direction

gadget a small tool or device with a clever design or unusual use

gamma ray a dangerous wave of energy

genetic mutation a change in a being before it is born that means it will look or act differently when it grows up

genius a person with an unusual ability to think or create

humanoid robots that have a human-like appearance or behavior

insane crazy

mineral a natural substance that comes from underground

nemesis someone that always works against you

radioactive giving off dangerous rays of energy

repulsor rays a weapon similar to a laser beam that can injure enemies

secret identity a disguise to hide who they really are

storyboard a series of images that tell a story

supernatural coming from outside the natural world

FURTHER INFORMATION

Books

DC Comics: The Ultimate Character Guide, Brandon Snider, Dorling Kindersley, 2011.

The Avengers: Earth's Mightiest Heroes, The Ultimate Character Guide, Alan Cowsill, DK Publishing, 2010.

The Shadow Masters (DC Super Heroes. Superman), Paul Kupperberg, Rick Burchett, & Lee Loughridge, Stone Arch Books, 2011.

Websites

Home of Marvel comics.
http://marvel.com/

Home of DC comics.
www.dccomics.com

Learn about all the different superheroes on the Superhero database.
www.superherodb.com/

TV Series

Look for these animated series on DVD to learn more about comic book superheroes.

Ben 10 (TV Series 2005–2007)

Fantastic Four
(TV Series 1994–1996, 2006–2007)

The Incredible Hulk
(TV Series 1996–1997)

Superman (TV Series 1996–2000)

Transformers (TV Series 1984–1987)

Wolverine and the X-Men
(TV Series 2008–2009)

X-Men: Evolution (TV Series 2000–2003)

INDEX